ANTHOLOGY OF POETRY BY YOUNG AMERICANS®

2005 EDITION
VOLUME XXI

Published by Anthology of Poetry, Inc.

Printed in the United States of America

To submit poems
for consideration in the year 2006 edition of the
Anthology of Poetry by Young Americans®,
go to: anthologyofpoetry.com or

Anthology of Poetry, Inc.
PO Box 698
Asheboro, NC 27204-0698

Authors responsible
for originality of poems submitted.

The Anthology of Poetry, Inc.
307 East Salisbury • P.O. Box 698
Asheboro, NC 27204-0698

Paperback ISBN: 1-883931-53-3
Hardback ISBN: 1-883931-52-5

As we turn the pages of this book, will we find poems you have written? If you are one of the poets published in this edition of *Anthology of Poetry by Young Americans®,* you are part of a great poetry experience and we're proud of you! You've cleverly used words, imagination and experiences to weave the magical tapestry of poetry. We've read thousands of poems created by students who are five and some who are eighteen, as well as all the ages in-between. In our eyes, you are the finest poets we've discovered this year!

For sixteen years we've been publishing the works of poets and young writers from across the U.S. Our mail-bags and e-mail boxes overflow with submissions, which we feel honored to receive. Donning our reading glasses we read every poem, sharing the best ones with the other editors. For many are just too wonderful not to share.

And in the end we choose a few of the ones we think our readers will enjoy most. Rhymes with great rhythms, interesting constructions and words that sing to us are a few of our criteria. When we go to print, this book represents not only the work of fine student writers, but also the nurturing and inspiration of the educators and parents who have enabled this writing.

Whether you're one of the authors, a teacher, friend, parent or family member, thank you for putting your energies into encouraging these young poets. And if you're reading this book for the first time, we challenge you to use the Anthology of Poetry forum to add excitement to your creative writing endeavors.

The Editors

WHISKEY

Loved by all
Purred when I
Pet your tummy

Old gray fur
Never
Made me frown

I miss your
Flimsy
Little gray tail

You're gone
Forever but
Still in my heart

Pictures of you
Help me
Get through
The day

I will never
Forget you

I will love you
Forever
And ever

Samantha J. Schmidt
Age: 11

Here I lay,
Away in such a lonesome place.
Waiting for someone
To come and take me,
To take me away,
Away from this so-called world,

This is not a world.
This is a place of all living evil.
A place that only one man rules.
A place that has never changed,
A place where I live.

Here I lay,
Still in a lonesome place,
Waiting alone,
To leave this place
And change the world.

Caroline Rose Horrigan
Age: 13

On an icy pond
Lonely mittens lie unloved
Through the bitter night

Brianna Downing
Age: 10

TRICK-OR-TREATING OR TEA!

I went trick-or-treating and then I went home.
When I got home my mom asked me, "Do you like tea?"
I said, "No, I do not like tea."
I see a cup of tea on the table
so I just went trick-or-treating again.
While I was trick-or-treating I thought about tea
so I went back home
and my mom said it was on the table
so I went to get my tea.
But I don't think I want my tea now
because I saw my dog's paw in my tea.
AHHHHH!
"Is today Saturday Mom?"
"Yes," said Mom.
"Yes, yes, yes, yes!" I said.
I was so happy, then I was nappy
so I fell asleep on my mom's lap.
Then I went to the beach.
I played with a crayon in the sand.

Nathaniel Voss
Age: 8

BUY A CANDY BAR, SAVE A LIFE

Roswell Park
Lung Cancer
"Let's have a chocolate sale!"

Chocolates delivered
Class hooked on sale
Announcements and poster
Committees needed

"Buy a candy bar, save a life!"

Day of sale
"Wow, profits high!"
Dollar donations keep coming

Two hundred dollars
In profit after
A fifteen minute sale

"Let's have another sale!"

Chocolates delivered
Class hooked on sale
Announcements and poster
Committees go to work

Day of second sale
"Wow, profits high!"
Dollar donations keep coming

"Buy a candy bar, save a life!"

Money counted
Total money,
Eight hundred eighty two dollars

Money presented
At Roswell
Picture taken
Heroic feeling in
My stomach

I believe
We had saved
Lives.

Brianna Bork
Age: 11

ONE DAY WHILE PLAYING CATCH

One day while playing catch,
I dove for the ball and fell.
I ripped my brand-new jeans--
Shhh! Please don't tell.

I know I'll get in trouble
If anyone tells my dad,
Because, if you want the honest truth,
That rip is really bad!

Lindsay Thomas
Age: 10

LEFT BEHIND

Being left behind
Makes me feel bad
My cousin and my sister
Are making me mad

They have the coolest teachers
They exclaim every day
They always come home
So happy and gay

They make the funniest jokes
Where I wish to laugh along
But I feel out of place
Like I'm singing the wrong song

I love them both
And I always will
But being left behind
Is an unwanted skill

Angeline Zilka
Age: 11

THE BUZZING FLY

Sitting at the picnic table
Looking at the sky
Down comes a buzzing fly
Flew around my head
WON'T go away
WHACK!
WHACK!
WHACK!
Using my hand with all my might
Still alive
Thought and thought
Didn't know what to do
I KNOW!
Run into the kitchen
Jump as high as I could
GOT IT!
WHACK!
WHACK!
WHACK!
With the fly swatter
Fly just lying there
Perfectly still
Good-bye
Buzzing sound

Kristin Paul
Age: 11

DEAR FRIEND

I opened the window to a beautiful dog
As I watched her jump so high and high
  after she tried so many times
I watched her look at all the cars as they passed
  and went speeding fast
I loved how she acted so pretty when that collar came on
  with all her bells jingling about
She loved when I walked in the door every day,
  she would run to me just like a child
  who hasn't seen their mother in a long time
I remember how she slept so silently every night
She was an angel when it came to ball
She was so good at every act she made
How much I loved her was a lot
At night I loved how she acted so sweet
Her little bells jingled every night and day
  until that car came and took her away
What a dear she was, I still remember her
  in my dreams every night and day

Samantha Saraceno
Age: 11

WATER-SKIING

Put on water skis
Scared as ever
Grab onto rope
Ready to try

The boat starts its engine
I put water skis parallel
Stand up for ten seconds
Then fall

It hurt
A lot
But I wanted
To try again

I kept my skis parallel
This time my knees were bent
The boat starts to go
I stand up
Again

Faster, scarier
I pick up speed

I was halfway around the lake
A boat quickly passes
Scared out of my mind
I fall

Lindsey LoGrippo
Age: 11

MY BEST FRIEND CODY

Blew a big test
thought Mom would ground
friend Cody comes over
tells me a joke
makes me cheer up
comes over to my house
later after school ends
easy to compromise with
to play PS2 games
and also play sports
friend is home bound
had an awesome time
best day ever with
my best friend Cody!

Michael Brandon Puntoriero
Age: 11

MATH

I don't get this math at all.
I wish math would take a fall.
You always have to get it right.
What if you have bad sight?
My teacher is so very mad,
I start to feel really sad.
I think I'll go home and ask my dad!

Mitchell R. Doherty
Age: 8

MISS MOLIK

Every day too at 9:20
Have Miss Molik
For social studies.

Blonde hair
Quite tall.

Getting married
In summer.

VERY ORGANIZED!!!

Not much homework
Given by her.

Can be mean
But, is not.

Have fun with
Miss Molik.

Don't want to leave
Miss Molik
At the end of the year.

But, I'll
Have to.

Patrick Wood
Age: 11

ACTING MAKES FRIENDSHIPS THAT WILL LAST A LIFETIME

Theatre
Camp
Two
Weeks in
August
Fun, friends,
But it
Did not last
Need to wait

A whole entire year

To see my friends
Again.

Cydney,
Kind
And funny
Generous,
Thoughtful,
A true friend.

Tyler, a REAL
Character,
Friends
To the end,
And
Always
Forgets
His
Snack!

Elizabeth,
Quiet,
But fun
I'll never
Forget her.

Dan,
Tall and a low,
Manly voice
Can always
Make you laugh.

Caroline,
Shy, but has
Enthusiasm
And emotion.

We all
Acted
Together
Playing
Different
Characters,
Yet taking
All
of
our
masks
off.

Laura Mikolajczyk
Age: 11

A TIME TO REMEMBER

All I saw were pictures
The buildings
Standing tall
Feeling
Sorrowful
In the house
Pictures of the tragedy
Up on the wall
Tapes of it happening
The plane
Hit the Tower
From then on we called it
The World Trade Center Disaster
My dad visited the site
I never did
It was on television
Soldiers did
What they could
September 11th
Was the day it happened
Tourists' site
From then on here
It is still in
Our memories
Because now
It is all clear
Afghanistan
Did it from jealousy
Our freedom,
Safety,

And money
We are all sad,
It stayed in our hearts
Now we're in
Afghanistan
Bombs and guns
Killing innocent people
Freedom isn't free
The loved are in
Our hearts
Today the soldiers stand tall in Iraq
GOD BLESS THE U.S.A.

Stephanie Lanza
Age: 11

ORANGE, YELLOW, AND GREEN

Orange, yellow, and green
Falling from the sky
That leaf happened to catch my eye
That red as rust
So beautiful and so dull

The stem is long
And brown like the tree branch it just fell off of

Soon the leaves will all fall off and winter will come
But that is another day

Michael Tyler Verrastro

AN UNPLEASANT GUEST

A scratching at the door
wondering what the scratching was
then goes away
the scratching comes back again
the scratching stays for a while
get
worried

Mom pounds on the door
scares away
look out the window
catch
glimpse

SKUNK
wondering why the skunk was at our door
thought the garbage is what made the skunk come
we took out the garbage
got scared
thought skunk would pop out
still wondering why the skunk was there

Dolly Goodman

MUD MAN

Floating softly towards the rim
Not knowing if it was going in

Closer and closer to the net
There was hope and there was fret

Suddenly there was a bing
The ball hit hard off the circular ring

Down it came with a sudden thud
Bouncing toward the murky mud

Sprinting quickly on the double
Trying to save it from messy trouble

With the ball in my hands
And a smile on my face
Running too fast
I could not stop the speedy chase

As I reached the grass
I felt a squish
I was stuck in mud
Like a big old fish

I did my best to save the ball
But on that day we both did fall . . .
In the mud!

Zachary Thomas
Age: 11

APPLE PEELER ATTACK

On summer vacation
I was peeling an apple
with an apple peeler
Ahhhhhh
Gushing blood
my nail fell off
Mmmooommm
Mom what should I do
Hurry up run to the bathroom
Blok
  Blok
    Blok
goes the blood in the toilet
I'll go get some cotton
from the bathroom upstairs
there we go now
we have to wait
until your fingers heal
Okay
Okay

Brandon Kandefer
Age: 11

TEAM LEADER

Waking up in the morning,
  ready to go.
Feeling so cheerful,
  you know!
I go practice with my friends,
  ready to play.
Joking around with my friends,
  getting them pumped!
As I start the game pitching,
  I feel so excited!
I play a lot of positions,
  know a lot of teams.
I am really competitive,
  watch out!
I'm coming into the game,
  to try my hardest!

Patrick Cary
Age: 11

GOOD NIGHT

The sky
Looks like its eyes are
Twitching,
The light is
Off but
On

The air, full of
The smells of
Leaves and smoke

The ground is moist
And full of
mud

It is warm but you can
See
Your breath in the
Frosty
Autumn
Air

The moon says
Good morning
But the sun says good night

Alexa Januchowski
Age: 11

COLLECTION

My collection is not very big,
Not very big at all.
This collection is of nutcrackers,
The size is from big to small.

Claire from the Nutcracker Ballet,
Is my favorite I do say.

I get one every Christmas Eve,
Put them in orderly fashion,
Then I leave.

The nutcracker that I got,
From my nana on the spot.
I got it from a college show,
That is all decorated with mistletoe.

I love my nutcrackers so much,
I keep them on a very, very, very high shelf!
So no one can touch them but . . .
ME!!

Elizabeth Ahl
Age: 11

DOING WHAT I LOVE TO DO

Flying
In the air

Zooming
  Down
Crazy Eights

My goggles
Protecting
My eyes

The wind
The snow
Blowing in
My face

I hit a bump
Go up
In the air
I swerve
I curve
And then
I fall

Then on
The chairlift
Twenty feet high
Let's do that again!

Flying
In the air

Touching
The sky

Mary Janak
Age: 11

HOCKEY

Puck drops
Get ready
They're coming
Oh no!
They shot the puck
The puck missed
Went into the corner
They passed the puck
They took another shot
I saved it
Cover it up said a teammate
I did it
There was a crowd around me
Everyone starts to push
Then an official comes in
Gets the puck
Then called a penalty
On the other team
Then the puck drops again

Brett Piatek
Age: 11

THE SEA AND ME

Nothing to do
Just relax
Me, happy
Me, joyful

Sparkling blue sea
Bright blue sea
The sun
Hitting against the surface of the water
So many colors
So much relaxation

This makes me forget
ALL problems
"Swooosshh"
The icy cold water
Rushes
Against my feet
No one can bother me
Just me, myself and the sea

Nothing to do
Just relax
Me, happy
Me, joyful

Watching the sunset
Makes me sad
To see the beautiful color
Fade away . . .

Nothing to do
Just relax
Me, happy
Me, joyful

Courtney Goodwin
Age: 11

WINTER

Cold out
bundled up
warm
playing in the snow
frostbite?
Scarf off
too tight on my neck
too tight
Snowman
snowboard
sledding
snow falling
Inside
hot cocoa
sweats on
drinking
nice and cozy
snow falling

Alyssa Gemmati
Age: 11

TRICK-OR-TREAT

I go out into the dark
With my friends right by my side
We go up to the doorstep
And a man is right inside

We then get lots of candy
And look at our great treat
We run around the neighborhood
Yelling, "Trick-or-treat"

I go to every doorstep
With my bag right in my hand
They drop in some candy bars
Isn't that just grand?

I later see some monsters
And goblins at the door
Yelling, "Trick-or-treat"
"More, more, more!"

Samantha Dirschberger
Age: 11

A WONDERFUL, WHITE, SPARKLING CREATION

The white snowflake
Slowly falls.
A piece of Heaven
Coming
Down
From above.

It goes

D D D D
O O O O
W W W W
N N N N

In a perfectly straight line.

Glimmering
And sparkling
All the way
D
O
W
N.

lands in a pile
it of
Until snow.

Victoria Luongo
Age: 11

WHERE POETRY HIDES

Poetry hides in a lot of places
Places you can't fully find
Poetry hides in places you can't reach,
Reach down deep,
This is what you'll find . . .

Poetry hides in your heart, with
emotion and hope

Poetry hides in your soul, with
things you love to do

Poetry hides in your mind, which
controls your every move

Poetry hides in your actions, with
the things you should and should not do

Poetry hides in your dreams, with
the hope of fulfilling them all

Poetry hides in you, you just have
to let it out

Jenna Wackowski
Age: 11

CAN'T FALL ASLEEP

Christmas Eve
Wondering
Waiting
Trying to
Sleep
Much too
Excited

Glancing
At the
Clock
Wishing I
Could
Speed up
Time

Closing
Eyes
Counting sheep

Much too
Excited
To fall
Asleep

Lindsey Nowak
Age: 11

SAMMY

I love the way he moves about
as a feather floating
D
O
W
N
from the sky
Through every crack and space
you see
Cute as a button
I have ever seen
Jumps around
twirls his tail
Playful
like a chimpanzee on a vine
Sits in your lap
so perfectly
As still as a string rolled up in a ball
Cozy and warm
Pet him every day
Soft as fuzzy pink slippers
His meow is so quiet and gentle
Like a lullaby that is sung to a baby
My one and only one
Most adorable thing
ever
That kitten
"SAMMY"

Alyssa Bliemeister
Age: 11

FLIGHT

When a bird flies
Overhead
No evidence
Of its passage
Is found

The light air
Lashed by
The beat of wings
And pierced by the
Cut of its talons

No sign
No presence
Of a bird
Overhead

Nothing to
Be found there
Anymore
Or ever again

Khristine Bryant
Age: 12

COMING ABOUT

I feel wind
blowing on my face.

The cold water from the lake
is splashing me.

I watch the sunset,
thinking how beautiful it is.

The boat is tipping
from side to side.

We glide on the water,
just my grandpa, the boat and I.

With the life jacket squeezed around me,
I feel so safe.

I feel a light rain
all around me.

My grandpa says
"Coming about"
and we head back to shore.

Lauren Ratajczak
Age: 11

MY DOG IS PSYCHO

My dog is psycho.
I love him a lot.
I chase him and chase him.
He never gets tired.

My dog is psycho.
I think something is wrong.
He never gets tired.
Not at all, all day long.

My dog is psycho.
He plays and plays.
He just does not stop.
He just does not sleep.

What do I do?
I love him a lot.
He just runs and runs
And just does not stop.

My dog is psycho.
He is too fast for me.
Why doesn't he just
Sleep?

MY DOG IS PSYCHO!

Zachary Patti
Age: 11

BASEBALL

I love baseball. It's really fun.
You hit and catch the ball.
I am an awesome pitcher, too.
And that is pretty much all.

Damon Fermo
Age: 10

MY GRANDPA AND I

The growing so tall,
The grass makes me laugh,
When I roll around,
Then my grandpa said,
"Work, work, work."

Then I say "Okay,"
So I went to work,
I had to mix the dirt,
And he did too.

When we were planting plants,
I saw a poppy,
Then I said, "Can I call you Poppy?"
Then he said, "Sure."

Mitchel Lochhead
Age: 11

HAMSTERS

I like hamsters,
I bet you do too.
They're very, very cuddly,
And you could name them Sue.

So I bet you'd want to have one,
That is as pretty as a beaut,
A cuddly, furry, snuggly one,
That's snuggled up so cute.

Melanie April Izard
Age: 7

BEST FRIENDS

Friends mean the world to us
Every single day,
Being the best friend
We could ever have,
But there is one friend
That is special in my heart.
She is always there for me,
Being the friend
Anyone could be.
Her name is
Stephanie Lanza.

Mary O'Shaughnessy
Age: 11

ROSWELL

Roswell Park,
Cancer,
Lungs,
“Let's sell candy bars.”

Chocolate,
Finally here,
A lot

Making
Poster groups,
And an
Announcement committee,

“Buy a candy bar, save a life.”

Fun
Occurring,
Good times,
Great memories,

Counted
Money,
Eight hundred eighty-two dollars,

YEA!!!

We
Beat our
Goal,
Which was
Five hundred dollars.

"Buy a candy bar, save a life."

Fun
Occurring,
Good times,
Great memories,

At that point
I
Felt like
I
Just saved
A million
Lives.

Sara Janovic
Age: 11

CATS

Cats are lovable.
Drooling means they are happy.
Ever adopted one?
Fun is their middle name!
Great friends.
Happy families have cats!
Intelligent animals they are!!

Emily Florczak
Age: 10

THE SPORT

Hard rubber ball,
Long metal sticks.
Padding,
Checking,
Sticks clinking,
Goals scored.
Everyone cheers!
Throwing the ball,
Passing.
Shooting,
Two quarters.
Twenty minutes each,
The game is over.
That is lacrosse.

Tyler D. Mallaber
Age: 11

MY DEAR BROTHER

My brother is annoying.
He picks on me all day.
He always talks.
He never listens to what I have to say.

My brother is annoying.
He never wants to play.
He and his friends ignore me.
I wish he'd go away.

My brother is annoying.
I don't know what to do.
But, I know he loves me.
And I know I love him too.

Michael Boyd
Age: 10

CHANCE

Such
a
small
child
so
cute
and
fun
three
four
five
years
have
passed
since
Chance
was
born.

Jacob Lorson
Age: 11

SWIMMING

Favorite sport
Level five
West Elementary

Love to dive
Never missed a class
Saturday at 1:00
It's such a blast!

I love this sport
Just love it!
Just love it!
Wonder if he will pick me
I hope for level six!

Emily McNiff
Age: 11

I CAN'T WAIT!

The warm sun of
Spring, beating down.

Green trees surrounded,
by beautiful
seas of color.

Easter is coming
and I can't wait!

The hot sun of
Summer, beating down.

Sandy beaches with
children
swimming and playing.

Independence Day
is coming
and I can't wait!

The cool breeze of
Fall, is blowing by.

Colorful leaves are
piled up in the yard.

Thanksgiving is coming
and I can't wait!

The cold wind of
Winter, is blowing by.

Beautiful blankets of white have
fallen.

Christmas is coming
and I can't wait!

Spring, summer,
Fall and winter.

Different seasons
throughout the year.

They all are coming
and I can't wait!

Devin Nicole Villagomez
Age: 11

AM I READY?

Why must I share?
hate it
it's not fair

friends have
their own room
but I don't

sister is nice
but
is annoying

can't wait until
April
sweet, sweet
April
when I get my own room

wait

am I ready
to sleep
downstairs
alone
downstairs

I wonder if
I'm ready
maybe
it's not so bad
to share

Alyse Stevenson
Age: 11

FALL LEAVES

Very messy
Hard to rake
Very boring
And not fun to get
Stuck in

Fun to drive in
Fun to jump in
When finished

Always fun with everyone

Daniel Boldt
Age: 11

STARTING SKATEBOARD

Bought a new skateboard at a store with Dad,
It was fifty dollars, Mom was mad

I got it autographed by a pro,
Got scratched up because I used it so

I replaced it with a new one
because it was very much used,
So I took it out of the garage
and with my room they were fused

Now there are stickers to cover the scratches,
Near that board I would never use any matches

Even though the skateboard is two years old,
It's still treated like a piece of gold.

Zachary Mazierski
Age: 11

ON THE BOARD

Riding along.
Going fast.
Wind in my face.
Ollies. Kickflips.

Grinding rails.
Heart is racing.
Going to get my friends.
Riding on tabletops.

In the skate park.
I'm going to the ramps.
Having so much fun.
On the board.

Lewis P. Lamonte Jr.
Age: 11

THE SOUNDS OF CHRISTMAS

Music being played
by the sounds of a
guitar
Song about Christmas

Chris Kattan
holding
a keyboard
turning his head
back and forth
"I don't care what your mommy says
Christmas time is neeauh"

Fred Armisen
dancing with
little movements
near keyboard

Jimmy Fallon
shaking maracas
"I don't care what your daddy says
Christmas time is neeauh"

Finesse Mitchell
standing there
doing nothing

Horatio Sanz
playing music
on his
guitar
"I wish it was Christmas today
I wish it was Christmas today"

Watching this
on TV
My mom and I
laughing hysterically
We thought these guys
were crazy
but funny

My favorite was
Chris Kattan
He made me laugh
the most

That was
the funniest skit
of the night
on SATURDAY NIGHT LIVE'S
CHRISTMAS SPECIAL

Michael Banko
Age: 11

DESERT PLANTS

Amazing plants
Green and sharp

All over
The mountains
Tall and slender

Bright white flower
Blooming on top
Right outside
Of our hotel room

Amazing plants
Green and sharp

Samantha Dalka
Age: 11

CRESCENT MOON

Sparkling in the darkness.
The harvest moon
Traps your spirit.
Feeling relaxed and rejoiced.

The stars glitter,
Red, yellow and blue.
So colorful,
Feeling dizzy, but happier.

Sparkling in the darkness
Shining bright.

Justin Huss
Age: 11

AN EXHAUSTING MORNING

Saturday morning
very chilly
the grass wet
and damp

I am very nervous
waiting for the whistle to blow
waiting for the boys to finish running
I wonder how I will do

The whistle blows
the girls are off

I make my way
around the soccer pole
already exhausted

Heading down the hill
feels like I am going to die

Around the basketball courts
wanting to collapse

Ran through some puddles
SPLASH

Heading for the finish line
exhausted
great accomplishment

Came in fifth place
so proud of myself.

Kristen Harrigan
Age: 11

FEED ME

Mom comes home
Tabby meowing nonstop
almost like saying
feed me, feed me
in little cat talk
Mom gets the food
Tabby following her
jumps on the counter
bowl fills up
Mom takes it to Tabby's
other food by the laundry room
Tabby following still meowing
Mom gives Tabby the food
Tabby gulps it down
and meows as if to say
thank you for feeding me

Adam Johnson
Age: 11

3/11/04

Two wonderful angels came down from Heaven
to bring laughter and joy and love to a family!
The time we had with them,
kicking and playing inside Mommy's tummy!
Are the memories that will last a lifetime.

They died in Mommy's tummy for only one reason!
The Lord missed them and wanted them home.
Although the pain of heartache came over us,
we'll still have to remember
our two little angels that God gave to us,
remember their little faces and big heads.
They had all their fingers and toes
just like Mommy and Daddy.

Though the time we had with them was short,
they'll be in our dreams and prayers forever!

In memory of Nathan James and Chandler Anthony.
(We love you!)

Michele Brickner
Age: 17

LAST NIGHT

Last night when I got under my blanket
It was as warm as a lion
Soft as a fluffy pillow
Comfortable as like I am in water
So relaxing that I would never wake up
Never-ending
All my sore bones felt better

Soon or later
Morning comes
Back to sore bones
Again
'Til
Next night

Cody Raiser
Age: 11

THAT TIME OF THE YEAR

All
dressed up in
red and
white.

In a
sled
with lots
of
toys
in the back.

Crowd
staring.

Reindeer tots
pulling
sled.

Nervous,
but
all right.

Sweating
because of
heat.

While the
fake snow
falls,
I hand out
Gifts
to children.

Proud.

Meet
Mrs. Claus
back at
home.

Kissed
on the
cheek.

Go to
sleep.

Preschool
Christmas
play.

Joe Kapuscinski
Age: 12

THE GIVER

I always liked her,
The Giver.

My friend,
Sure loved her,
Like a sister.

Shrimpy,
Her home name.

Liked it best,
When she would laugh.

She was a real,
Giver.

Never gave a thought,
About lending someone a token.

Caring,
She was always
Caring.

Every intention of hers,
Care about the others.

The Giver,
Definitely,
The Giver.

Always and forever,
My friend,
The Giver!

Nicole Dalka
Age: 11

Bears
little cubs
runs very fast
loves the cool water
Bears

Thomas M. Catapano
Age: 9

THE MONTHS

January
Oh, the winter is fine!
February
Who will be my valentine?
March
Will St. Patrick bring you a pot of gold?
April
Soon it should stop being so cold.
May
The flowers are in bloom.
June
School will be out very soon.
July
Boom, Crack, Boom, it's Fourth of July.
August
Summer vacation is almost done--Oh my!
September
We're back in school.
October
Halloween will be so cool!
November
Thanksgiving mashed potatoes--yum!
December
Christmas is here.
Pa rum pa pum pum, me and my drum.

Alyriana Boughton
Age: 10

LIBERTY

Dull copper with flecks of green,
Woman of welcome,
Her name means be free,
Liberty

In the harbor she stands greeting,
Awaiting the newcomers of America,
The tablet telling of the freedom to come,
Liberty

Mother of the poor,
Door to America
But where is the key?
A crown so perfectly perched on her head,
Seven seas, seven points,
The road we have traveled,
Liberty

Her foot enchained,
Yearning to be free,
Stepping forward to freedom,
Liberty

She stands alone
Yet welcomes with the strength of many,
Liberty

Jeffrey Mills
Age: 12

WHITE

White is quite a sight,
It's very, very bright,
It's soft, gentle, and light
And oh, how happy it is to see that sight!

White sounds mellow,
Sort of like Jell-O,
Fluffy and puffy,
Like his white marshmallow.

White smells full of delight,
Like sugarplums at night,
Soft and sweet,
My shoes come off my feet.

White tastes like milk,
With 100% silk,
Eggs, eggnog, marshmallows, and white M&M's,
Are all good for white on a wintry night.

When I touch white,
I feel a frostbite,
Giving me chills in the moonlight,
Despite my fight on a wintry night.

James M. Dorman
Age: 9

LEAVES

Burning leaves,
Colored fire.
With great ease,
Descend to mire.
Floating gently,
On the wind.
Falling swiftly,
Gently landing.

Emily Wallmann
Age: 10

WINTER

Winter is quiet,
Except for an occasional snowball riot.
Winter is cold,
Which is what most don't desire,
So, that's why most stay by the fire.
Winter for me is fun,
There are many things to be done.
Like snow shoveling, shopping, putting up lights,
And wrapping gifts for the Holy Night.
Even though winter will soon be done,
I know next winter will still be fun.

Nicholas Merenda
Age: 11

THE SECOND DARKNESS WILL NEVER BE

They were just four hobbits,
But were told to set off on a quest,
To bring the ring to Mordor to destroy it,
Even though they weren't the best.

One ring, nine companions,
Off to Mordor they went,
But they all split up in groups,
And the whole land stirred.

Frodo and Sam were left with the ring,
Gollum as their guide,
Such a nasty little thing.
They ditched him and destroyed the ring,
Went to Gondor and bowed before the king.

King Aragorn said, "You bow to no one.
We shall bow to you."
Then he bowed down and his people bowed, too.
The hobbits felt special,
As special as can be,
And all were happy again.
They knew a second darkness would never be.

Ashley DeNardo
Age: 10

Hockey
moving fast
skating up ice
He shoots he scores
Hockey

Nathan Hellstern
Age: 9

Dogs
best friend
loving, caring, playing
walk, nice, run, cute
walking, playing, running
playful, considerate
Katie

Victoria Frankiewich
Age: 9

SECRET COVE

Alone in the dark,
Just my brother and I.
Standing there silently,
Just my brother and I.

He then dives in,
I soon follow.
The sweet salty air,
I sniff, then swallow.

Our secret cove,
Covered in by mist.
We come each night,
I always insist.

The only light,
Is the silver moon.
It's not very early,
I hope morning doesn't come soon.

As I dive in,
I feel great joy.
I don't think I can ever be sad,
Because I feel like God's toy.

A secret cove,
Wouldn't be fun,
Without my dear brother,
Yes, he's the one.

The water reflects,
Our two shapes.
His and mine,
I caught it all on two tapes.

Our secret cove,
What a special place.
Our secret home,
Our secret space.

Margaret Casler
Age: 11

Horse
cute, friendly
jumps, runs, walks
loves oats and carrots
Horse

Victoria Vazzana
Age: 9

F all is so cool
A corns fall down in fall
L aughs can be heard
L eaves are raked in piles

Alexandra Samsonik
Age: 9

Soccer
awesome, cool
running, kicking, scoring
What a fantastic game!
dribbling, screaming
fun, great
Goals

Emma Falk
Age: 9

FALL

F alling leaves come off the trees.
A utumn is finally here.
L ovely smell of pumpkin pies.
L ovely moon bright at night.

FALL

Kate Brooker
Age: 9

They're
orange
and green like
outer space. They smile
and gleam like your face.
Pumpkins are round
like your plate.

Kiely Gagnier
Age: 9

THUMP!

Bump!

OWW!
I now have a bump on my head
from the thump of the basketball.

My head feels like a thousand needles
popping a balloon.

This is not anything new.
I am ALWAYS getting hit in the head.
That is why my head is always red.

It is all the basketball's fault.
The basketball is the one chasing me.
If only it would go in the hoop.

I am thinking that the basketball doesn't like me.
Why won't the ball just let me be?

Running, racing, retrieving the basketball.
Running, racing, retrieving I didn't want to fall.

The bouncing, bothersome, basketball
is finally going away.

Sarah Lynn Grossman

likes M ummies
A lligators too
L oves outdoors
C old in winter
warm in O ctober
L oves the summer
M alcolm is special

Malcolm Rieck
Age: 9

M y favorite thing is shopping
O ntario is my favorite lake
L oving and caring
L aughs a ton
Y ells and screams a lot

Molly Bell
Age: 9

AUTUMN

Colors floating in the air,
like a tornado whirling 'round.
Each leaf is so, so fragile,
just like a glass cup.
Autumn is when there is a chill,
then soon the snow will flurry.
Frost will crawl up your spine,
and the breath you see fades away.

Katelyn Trieskey
Age: 10

J oy
A mazing
C ool
K reative
-
O dd
-
L azy
A wesome
N oble
T rick-or-treat
E vil
R ound
N eat

Quinten Rock
Age: 9

FRIENDSHIP

Friendship is like love
forming every day
people get together
in a special way
friendship is like love
can't you see friends
forever to catch you
when you fall
friendship is love
pure love

Colleen Lazzara
Age: 10

THE TRUTH

In present times,
I have come to find

That people nowadays,
Have changed their ways

For now our wants are our needs,
And we can't survive much longer

But when our needs become our wants,
Indeed we will grow stronger

Craig Carlisle

SISTERS

Prissy, Jenny and also me
we are sisters all three.
No person or distance
can take away what we share,
or who we are,
because we are connected to each other,
bonded with a special kind of glue
called sisterly love;
it's plain to see.

Dedicated to Prissy and Jenny

Carley L. Connor
Age: 10

K atie is funny.
A rts and crafts.
T ime is running out.
I love the world.
E verybody's a winner.

Katie Ruberti
Age: 9

F all is here with lots of leaves.
A utumn brings a pleasant breeze.
L eaves are falling off of trees.
L et's be thankful for all of these.

Kelly Julia Smith
Age: 9

e X tra fun
never M ad
        A lways having fun
        S nowing all the time

Blake Owens
Age: 9

SUNSET

As I lay upon my
Porch
In a swing watching
Watching
What some call God's
Masterpiece
I call it a piece of
The world
Some may be lost
In what is being said
I simplify to what everyone
Can understand
What I wrote
A matter of words
Is nonetheless a
SUNSET
If you think a little
You will find a
SUNSET
Is a sign
A sign of peace
Or maybe a
Sign
Of love
Depending on your view of things
What is a world
Without a
SUNSET

Brendan King
Age: 10

A FRIEND

Who falls behind is left behind . . . that's what they say
A bit of hope; joy; courage
A rose so silky may represent pain
Although friendship befalls like sprinkles of rain
An owl has eyes only strong enough for truth
Ye lurks around every corner so don't trip and don't run
People have hearts that are slimy as a snail
So don't let it leave a trail, all over your heart
It could last you a lifetime
What lies behind a closed door
Can represent life or death
A closed door is always a secret
And will remain a secret until you open it
Everyone is different, just like the sea and the sand
But between them they are alike
Because they go hand in hand
Together they are the beach, just like a light bulb
Puts light and dark hand in hand
Don't be alone with all shame; just make a friend . . .
Anyone can.

Tianna Negrón
Age: 11

A NIGHT IN THE FOREST

Pitching up the tent in the darkness of the night
The pounding of the stake in the ground
echoing through the forest
The atmosphere around me, jet-black and musty
With only the forlorn glow of the moon
The moon drenched the cold earth with silver
The sheen glowing like the light of a candle
As flames emerged from my two rubbing sticks
I let out a gasp and the blazing fire grew in front of me
The mellow crackling perturbing the ongoing silence
The marshmallow on my lanky stick
turning a soft golden brown
A sweet smell wafting towards me
The soft substance expanding with every gooey bite
The starry sky hovering over the world below
And an icy cold wind swirling around me
As the sky grew darker, I put out my fire
And drifted off to sleep underneath the luminous stars
The tree branches drooping down
as if protecting me from the dangers of the night

Brianna Miele
Age: 12

BASEBALL

Sound of bat cracking,
ball soaring over the fence,
wooden bat collapses to the ground,
pitcher looks tired, fatigued,
call to the bull pen,
the crowd starts the wave,
the home team coming back,
scoreboard was 5 to 0,
and was changed to 5 to 3,
player getting pounded at the plate,
players slapping him on the back,
singles, doubles, triples, home runs,
walks, strikeouts, outs, fly outs,
grounder, line drive, pop up, blooper,
home run, home run, home run, home run,
grand slam flashes on the screen,
the home team has come back,
the crowd screams,
the game is over,
done, gone, finished,
baseball is the game for the ages

Dominick Rodriguez
Age: 12

FISHING WITH BOPA

Tackle boxes, hooks, bobbers and more
Tangled up poles and fish galore
Nothing to think of, no problems at all
Just miles of goldenrod standing up tall
One fish after another, tags on my line
Not a time to be home, the day was all mine
About one o'clock the bites got too few
It was time to eat lunch, just us two
Bopa and I cracking jokes one after the other
When the cell phone rang, on the line was Mother
Be home for dinner, and for dessert we'll have pie
But we wanted to fish more so we made up a lie
The rest of the day ran pretty smoothly
A big 'un here and there, it was all too soothing
By four o'clock we only had three minnies to spare
Everyone left but the mosquitoes in the air
The fish stopped biting and the night got cool
But even the worst day of fishing
  beats the best day of school

Brooke Hnatyszyn
Age: 12

When flakes of white fall from the sky
They're packed together, soaring high
Mittens go on as snow and humans meet
There's no time to stop and take a seat
A shovel of snow is dumped on a girl
As snowballs through the air will whirl
Boys against girls, they'll fight it out
The air is filled with laughter and shouts
After hours of fun it must come to an end
And the enemies are now once again friends

Julia Eppehimer
Age: 12

P layful
I ntelligent
G iggly
G ross
Y ummy
S loppy

=

C uddly
U seful
T wo-toed
E xcellent friends

Casey Nowicki
Age: 11

As I sit in the light of the sun,
and listen to the birds sing, the winds blow,
the leaves shake on the trees,
and watch them sway in the breath of the breeze.

Kira Jasmine Gottlieb
Age: 9

THE BAT

If I were a bat
I'd wear a black hat
On Halloween night
I'd like to cause a lot of fright!!!
Everyone will scream and run with dear life
at my sight!!!
Afraid I will bite!!!
All I want to say is good night!!!

Trisha Moritz
Age: 9

Sunset comes up,
Birds are chirping,
I open my eyes
And say five more minutes.

Lidia Carangi
Age: 11

APPLE PIE

This time of year apples are ripe.
The apples are spiced with cinnamon and spice.
The apple pie is great!
It is gone in a blink of an eye!

McKenzie J. Martin
Age: 9

FIREWORKS

Red purple orange and green
They were the best fireworks I've ever seen.
Pink yellow white and blue
Higher and higher they all flew.
Bang--Boom Bang--Boom
Explosions
And shapes like a mushroom.
On my blanket I sat and gazed
As my summer faded away.

Olivia Ann Zabrodsky
Age: 9

IF I WAS SPACE

If I was space I would be very dark
I would have planets
I would have astronauts on me
I would have lots of stars
I would have the Big Dipper
If I was space I would feel out of this world.

Jordan Johnson
Age: 9

THE WHOLE YEAR

The crisp, cold autumn day.
The freezing, frosty winter day.
Then summer is the time to play.
Do you know how fast seasons pass away?

Logan Hickman
Age: 7

FALL LEAVES

Fall leaves falling off the trees
in the cold and windy breeze.
In the fall we rake them all orange, yellow, and red.
And put them in a pile and make them into a bed.
Fall is the season for pumpkins
and lots of leaves to jump in.

Nicholas Tobias
Age: 9

THE WIND

I swirl through the trees.
I am the wind.

I dance with the thunder.
I am the wind.

I howl when I'm mad.
I am the wind.

I'll blow towards you.
I am the wind.

Kaitlyn Stebbins
Age: 7

THE CAT

I have a cat,
She's really fat.
She scratched a bear,
And put a tear.
My cat had a ball,
She made it fall.
Her hair is brown,
She does not frown.

Linnzi Marie Milliman
Age: 9

WIND IN WINTER

When it's freezing
I blow frost crystals.
When it's cold
I shake bare trees.
When it snows
I swirl the snowflakes.
Watch out
Or I'll blow cold on you!
I am the WIND!

Abigail Johnson
Age: 7

FALL CHANGES

In fall the leaves fill the ground.
Yellow, red, and orange in gigantic mounds.
Trees go bare.
Like a grandpa losing his hair.
Pretty soon there will be no leaves.
Then snow will cover the trees.

Alizé Scott
Age: 9

MY MIRROR

How do we know that
The world
Really is how it looks?
How do we know that
Our eyes
Aren't fooling us?
Have we been seeing?
False images
All our lives?
Maybe we have been living
What we would call a
Lie,
But how untrue is it?
We have been taught
To depend on what things
Look like
Rather than what they
Say or do.
So, what if the world really
IS
Like the image my mirror portrays?
Then maybe
The most important question of all is . . .
Does
It
Matter?

Faith Benson
Age: 12

MY KITTEN

My kitten's name is Socks.
Don't let the name fool you.
You wouldn't want to
wear her on your feet!
She is wild, not at all tame.
Socks spitters-spatters
when you pet her.
If Socks has nine lives,
she's spent most of them!
My kitten is
adorable and cute.
She is tan, gray and white.
Socks has teensy, tiny paws
and she uses them to drink milk.
She even gets milk mustaches.
Moles and mice beware!
She'll catch you if she can and then
leaves them for me as gifts.
Not exactly what I had in mind!
Each and every day could be my birthday.
Each and every day could be Christmas.
With a cat like Socks I guess
I never really know.

Kayla M. Anderson
Age: 9

A SORRY ROUTINE

Bruises all over,
Irritable and bored,
You went to the doctor for what
Was a routine checkup,
As it turned out, it was not.

He took your blood,
Frowned, and told you
To go straight to the hospital!

Your friends are worried,
Your family concerned,
To see that you,
A sunny three-year-old,
Has a scary disease.

"Boo-Boo" you call it,
"Leukemia," they say.
May a normal life resume again one day.

Weakened from chemo,
Stuck in a bed,
"Why, oh why her," many have said.

Roses attempt
To brighten your room,
Stuffed bears and dolls to comfort you.

Alive with fever,
A result of the infection,
And doctors fill your veins with injections.

Now you go home,
For a short while,
Before you must return,
To ensure that you're fine.

Life is too frail
To fight long against death,
Caroline, dear cousin,
I pray you will live.

Sarah Harms
Age: 14

BLACK ANT

Black ant, black ant, o' how you work
Black ant, black ant, how much you're worth
Working hard in the sun
Never stopping 'til the job is done
Never complaining or taking a break
Never giving up for the colony's sake
Black ant, black ant, carry the food
Black ant, black ant, quickly before noon
Hurry, hurry winter is coming
Hurry, hurry quietly humming
Black ant, black ant, work so hard
Black ant, black ant, living in my yard
You taught me a lesson, can't you see?
Work hard and sting work like a bee.

Ryan Maxson
Age: 12

THE INCREDIBLE EXPERIENCE

We turn off from the dusty dirt road.
We see some horses in the field.
Frolicking, grazing, running, chasing.
The cold nips my nose
As we walk up to the barn.
We stop to admire the view.
Brown, red, yellow, and orange leaves cover the hillside
Blending together as one.
One tree, one leaf, one hill, one view.
One magnificent view.
We carry on.
Trying to reach the protection of the barn.
We reach the warm and inviting smells of the barn.
We walk into the indoor and are greeted
By the soft whinnies of the horses as usual.
We venture through the barn.
Looking, seeking, hoping, trying
To locate the instructor.
We split up.
I find my horse.
She finds the instructor.
We all meet by the crossties
Just as I finish up.
Then we head to the arena rein in hand.
Ready for an incredible experience.

Skyler Harwood
Age: 12

Dear teacher,

I know you're my teacher,
But you're not my teacher to me.

You're a fairy of some sort
That grants every wish.
You're that deep-sea diver
That shares her treasure.

I know you're my teacher . . .
BUT YOU'RE MY BEST FRIEND TO ME!

Laura Knighton
Age: 9

A CITY STREET

A city street has cars on the highway.
A city street has tall buildings and small buildings.
In a city street there are kids picking flowers.
In a city street there are some animals but not a lot.
In a city street there are people shopping
and looking for new cars.
I like the city street because there're a lot of things to do.

Sierra Nelson
Age: 9

SNOWFLAKES

Snowflakes can be all shapes, all sizes.
And snowflakes can be any design you can imagine.
Round, circular, oblong, rectangular.
But one thing snowflakes cannot be
is any color but white.
Because that's the color of snow.
I like snowflakes.
They can fit my personality.
And you might like them, too.
Snowflakes are beautiful!

Caitlyn Miles
Age: 11

AMERICA

Right here on this spot
People have cried
Because people have fought
And people have died
But the flag still hangs
High in the air
Put peace in the nation
That's what people share
Put peace in the country
But is it still here?

MaryClaire Fiacco
Age: 9

AUTUMN

Autumn, a beautiful time,
the brilliant colors.

The constant sound of geese
as they fly south
on wings of the V.

The hills turn red, orange, and yellow.
It is truly
and undoubtedly beautiful.

Autumn and its beauty.
The whole experience of it
surrounds me.

The wind blows,
thousands of bright and colorful leaves find me
and surround me in a twister of color.

The leaves float slowly to the water.
They land so lightly
that the ripples disappear almost instantly.

Autumn can be reflected in a lake
of beauty, love, and friendship.

Can you?

Alissa Jolley
Age: 12

Leaves rustling
People singing
This is the sound of adventure
Blowing flowers
Lazily dance
This is the smell of adventure
Trees around
Animals' bliss
This is the look of adventure
Wind
Hitting your face
Stroking your hair
This is the feel of adventure

Edward Scott - Koa Thompson
Age: 13

FINGERS

Little funny finger
Why aren't you a singer
Big fat thumb
Why are you so dumb
My tiny little pinkie
I'm going to call you Twinkie
Middle finger bad
You make me sad

Keaton Mickulesku
Age: 12

BIRDS FLYING BY

Birds flying by me
soaring through the wind.
Quite soft sounds
with bells ringing in my heart.
Time for bed
I dare not speak.
Before I go in I hear nothing
but just one little peep.

Megan Warriner

TRAPPED

I've been trapped inside
For so very long
I feel like I must run
Run away and hide
Nobody notices me
Nobody can hear me
I'm trapped
Backed into a corner
Hiding from outside life
Someday soon I'm sure
I'll break free

Ashley M. Pabis
Age: 12

A HUG

A hug from your mom
Is like the sun
On a cold winter's day
It warms you up
And makes you feel safe
A hug is the world
Turning slowly and quietly below you
As the world keeps spinning
Your hug is everlasting
Until it finally stops
And your hug comes to an end
But you know you can't wait
Until the next time
When you get the everlasting hug back
And the world starts to spin
Slowly and quietly
Underneath you again

Sarah Fick
Age: 12

NATURE

The flowers and the trees,
the grass and leaves,
this is nature.

Alex Campanis
Age: 11

STANDING THERE

There you were standing on an empty, silent road,
waiting for someone to come.
You screamed, "Help!" as loud as you could,
but no one answered.
You waited for a while,
still no one showed up.
You were standing there alone.

Melissa Lucey
Age: 12

BUTTERFLIES

Butterflies are beautiful.
They flutter in the skies.
Out in the meadows, they peacefully glide.
Butterflies are beautiful.
They flutter in the skies.

Tatiana Beer
Age: 11

CHRISTMAS

Heavy sparkling blankets of snow
cover the trees in the night.
Soft winds blow at the crack of dawn.
Light bursts through the glass window
on our Christmas tree,
the ornaments sparkling like Heaven!
Church bells ring like an angel's song.

Jessica Pease
Age: 10

PATH OF SORROW

I walk down the path of sorrow
with no one to guide my way.
I'll probably get there by tomorrow
with a pocketful of heartbreaks.
There are changes all around me,
but yet you stay the same.
The way you break my lonely heart
and leave me with the blame.
The sun is shining brightly, but I still can't feel the flame
As I walk down my path of sorrow.
As the path winds with every confusing turn,
there are some lessons I have not learned.
As the trees scream and branches break,
I keep going with every sad step
I take as I walk down my path of sorrow,
I hear the wind as if it is crying my name.
I feel like someone is playing with my head
as if I am in some kind of game.
As I walk down my path of sorrow,
the flowers die with every step I take,
and I feel as though my life is at stake.
No one is here to help me or to get rid of my fears.
How long will I be here, how many years?
Another day is tomorrow
to see if I am still stuck in my path of sorrow.

Olivia Lusk
Age: 14

THE COMMA

The Lord said, “I AM, Moses.”
Yes--the very words of God.
You should thank Him there's a comma,
For wouldn't it be odd
If he had been so careless
To omit without a cause
That little arch of import
That signifies a pause?

For if the Sovereign Power,
As no one now supposes,
Had only said, without ado
Just simply, “I am Moses,”
The captives still would not be free,
The earth in whole would cease to be,
There'd be no bell of liberty,
And the Kingdom would not come, you see.

Such a little, unassuming thing
As a comma bears great worth,
And echoes through the ages
Of society's rebirth.
They are infinitely vital
To everything, and so,
Don't you dare forget them--
They could change the world, you know.

Now the sun can dazzle on the lea,
The moon can pull in tides at sea,
The English now can sip their tea.
And since you're nigh through reading me,
I hope that you'll return to see
My thoughts on the apostrophe.

Chelsea Lynn Kolz
Age: 13

IN MY MIND

The white tapestries in my mind,
the people o' so kind,
and in the moonlight, the day is spent,
but the next day will come, without a dent,
the red rug so keen and kind
and perfectly in line.
The bed is nice and sweet without a drop of sorrow,
you don't even have to borrow
a drop of this or a drop of that.
All you need is a tip of the hat.

Emma Plotkin
Age: 9

A NEW WORLD'S CREATION

The one revealed the theme.
And all the choirs sang.
With voices like great, but gentle beings.

It began with the feeling of heights,
of air, of cool, clean waters,
of growth and beginnings.
Of silent forests, bright lights,
and all things peaceful and graceful.

And then the ambitious one sang,
of all things cruel and cold.
Uncouth cacophonies and vain sounds.

Then all was calm.
Next, the discord arose
and was ever more cruel and cold.
Betraying, revealing, ravaging and imprisoning,
the chain that binds and holds.

Finally, the Great One rose, and for the last,
calmed the evil sounds.

And the theme was revealed,
of all the World's great creation.

But the land was blemished by the evil one's discord,
yet, nonetheless, the World was beautiful.
Just as the Great One conceived.

And the entire World slept.

An interpretation of J.R.R. Tolkien's story, The Ainulindale

Patrick James Ryan
Age: 11

THE CHICKEN

The chicken bawks all day.
The chicken can jump high.
The chicken can glide.
The chicken can run fast.
The chicken has wings.
The chicken is good to eat.
The chicken likes me.

Max Gaeta
Age: 8

LITTLE HERO

This little boy stands outside
Staring at his home
Engulfed in flames
Mother inside
Fearful thoughts
Race through his mind
Memories pass by also
Of a television show once watched
With a hero who rushes into the flames
Of a burning house
To save a family
From a flame-filled doom
He decides
To be this
Hero, running inside
To his mother's aid
Father at work
He's the man now
He stands big and tall
He runs inside through the door
Into the flames
All that is heard
Are shouts and screams
Of a terrified crowd
Standing and watching
This little boy
Running into certain doom
Minutes pass
Crowd is quiet
As it seems like hours
Then a figure appears
Through the smoke

Who'd have thought
It was the little boy
Mother at side, he drags and tugs
To pull her to safety
In the other hand he grips
His beloved teddy
What a sight
What a sight
Would have been a deadly night
If it weren't for that little boy
With an age of but six
With the dream of being that hero
With the thought of saving his mother
Who'd have thought a little boy
At the mere age of six
Considered a hero for the rest
Of his life
Always with the memory
Of the crowd
Of the flames
And of an unconscious mother
And of the television show
These memories will change his life
A lesson this mother learned . . .
Size does not matter

Dustin Taylor
Age: 14

BIG AND GRAY

Mommy had me yesterday, yesterday, yesterday
Mommy had me yesterday
I was big and gray.

I could not fit in the door, in the door, in the door
I could not fit in the door
I was really big.

How about my dumbo ears, dumbo ears, dumbo ears
How about my dumbo ears
And my big long trunk?

Guess what I am am am, am am am, am am am
Guess what I am am am
Guess what I am please.

Andrew VanFleet
Age: 10

Left right
Up down
Upside down
And all around
Having fun is my game
Roller coaster is my name

Eric M. Stickler
Age: 13

MY SNOWMAN

Look outside,
there's my snowman big and wide,
with a carrot nose
and arms made of wood.
Man, he sure looks really good.
Made of snow,
I wonder where he will go,
when he melts away someday.

Briannyn Payne

IT COMES AND GOES

Spring comes and spring goes
The flower sprouts and grows
Suntan lotion on your nose
All sidewalks are unfroze

Walking through the meadow grass
Swimsuits . . . the color of brass
Bugs all around . . . especially gnats

Out comes the deer
As it pokes out its ear
For it's in fear
And checking to see if spring is here.

Aimee Austin and Leann Green
Ages: 11

MY CAT

My cat is very big
like the fat cat Garfield.
He likes catching food for kittens,
but they do not have any mittens.
His name is Seymour Dolittle.
He is very funny.

Wileen Baker

MY FLUTE

My flute and I are best friends.
I play my flute like Toot, Toot, Toot!
I play my flute through the night.
I even play it in the light.

People even say I am crazy
but I'm even more lazy with it.
I watch my music when I play.
I'll still play it when it's May.
I love playing my flute.

Holly M. Willis

CHRISTMASTIME

Christmas is the time of year
to spread love, joy, happiness, and cheer.

From hanging ornaments on the tree.
Building snowmen for all to see.

Singing Christmas carols in the snow
while Jack Frost nips at your nose.

Sipping hot cocoa by the fire,
gazing at the mantle I admire.

As you see out the window the new-fallen snow,
you sense that Christmas is near.
In the distance ringing bells you hear.

As we fall to rest under the tree,
feeling all the happiness and Christmas glee.
Can't forget to set out milk and cookies for Santa to see.

Slowly we stumble to bed
with visions of sugarplums dancing in our head.

Turn off the light
for a long Christmas night.

Charlene M. Arena
Age: 10

L iving
O ut
V ows
I n
N ever-ending
G race

Jordan Neusch
Age: 10

COMPLETE

Our life is just beginning as two instead of one,
we already have gone through so many things
and there are many still to come.
Our love for each other will help us grow in the future
as two instead of one.
I will be there no matter what life brings
the good, the bad, and everything in-between.
You are my sun that shines so bright,
and you are my moon that lights my way at night,
the flowers in my heart, and the joy of my day.
When I sleep at night I think of you.
When I wake in the morning to see you by my side,
I am the luckiest girl alive.
The magic you have brought into my life
can't be explained.
I hold it close to my heart on locks and chains.
Today will bring only joy to both of us
for now we are complete with each other by our side.

Erica Peckham
Age: 14

MY DOG

Dog.
cute vicious.
snaps bites growls.
I love my dog.
Puppy.

AnnaMarie Marsilio
Age: 11

SUNDAYS

From a Sunday Mass,
 To a soccer pass.
From the car's last jerks,
 As nighttime lurks.
From a late night movie,
 To the final sips of my strawberry Smoothie.
From thinking of the days ahead,
 To going straight to bed.
Good night Sunday!
 Good morning Monday!

Jamie Lynn Post
Age: 13

Christmas
joyful, sparkly
sing, bake, share
Family and friends gather
Birth

Molly Bell
Age: 11

NOT ONLY A CHILD

A child is important
They're the future of tomorrow

What a child says and does
Could change your life forever

A child can bring a smile
To almost anyone's face

When a child is near
There is never any fear

You're only a child on the outside
For just a small amount of time

But the child inside of you
Can reach out anytime

Elizabeth Wenneman
Age: 11

THE BEAUTY OF FALL

Seeing the leaves change color, orange, yellow, red,
Viewed through the window, all snug in bed.
Shorts and tees are packed away,
Jackets and scarves are used for play.
Leaves blown on the ground,
Create a rustling sound.
All raked in a pile,
Kids jumping with a smile!
Geese and ducks flying south,
Before winter's blowing mouth.
A tall fire blazing at night,
Warm blankets, wrapped up tight.

Alyssa Topolski
Age: 10

Christmas
joyful, merry
laughing, unwrapping, feasting
Jesus Christ is born
Noel

Taylor Belcastro
Age: 11

LOVE

My life
happiness, peace
playing, learning, loving
Love is strong feelings
My world

Adeline L. DeSalle
Age: 11

Me
funny, big
eating, breathing, playing
I am really hysterical.
Child

Gino Sabatini
Age: 10

America
hope freedom
voting learning praying
I love our America
Country

Alison Colangelo
Age: 10

THE POEM

I had to write a poem.
The thing I knew I'd dread.
I thought it would be awful with visions in my head.
I wouldn't let it get me down because I knew I could.
In that moment on that day I really knew I would.

Mackenzie Gabriel Thomas
Age: 10

LIVED TO LAST

For the minutes of this one symphony
All the world is beautiful
The souls of the hungry
If not their aching bellies
Are quenched with song of the violin.

Perhaps there are those of us born
To be watchers,
Listeners,
Scribes
And perhaps centuries ago
There were those that lived to tell
Lived to last
Lived to whisper these melodies
Into the ears of our imaginations
So that we might
Run wild
With their notes,
Their measures,
Their movements.

I fear that I am born
To be a watcher
A listener
A scribe.
One who chooses the pens with which
We mark down this splendor
A wary eavesdropper
Along the corridors
Of the concerto
Try as I might with a pen
To harvest what Schubert has

On the wavering
String
Of the cello
I am halted, awe-struck, in my ascent
Certain that any attempt to reach such heights
Would be the kiss of inspired hubris.

I am a vase of souvenirs
Souvenirs of the artists
That created art
When art
Drew trills from Paganini.
Ah, I wish I'd lived in the streets
Of Mozart
Perhaps with his music as my muse
I might paint a song of his promise to me
In the language of silk, sunset sonatas
In the most resonant, echoing tunnel of my soul.

Bari Berger
Age: 16

CHEERLEADING

Sheer happiness is all I feel
While on a mat or on a field
I'm full of pride and joy
While I'm cheering on our boys
Just to make that one last score
Then to go and get some more
'Cause it's more than just short skirts
Sometimes it actually hurts!
Then for someone to retort
"Cheerleading is not a sport!"
"They stand around."
"That's all they do."
You don't know me very well do you?!
You see us flip and jump and dance
But there're things you don't see at a glance
Like pain from practice the other night
And bruises up our arms
That's right!
From basket tosses and overworked muscles
Yet, still through all the hustle and bustle
We look overjoyed
We keep our pride
'Cause we really love it
Deep inside
So listen up!
Now all of you!
I'm a cheerleader
It's what I do.

Sara Ann Deppenbrook
Age: 13

THE LAKE DAYS

I go every summer,
The calm wind blows,
I sit on my deck,
I long to jump in the lake,
Instead I get up.
I start to climb,
I get to the top,
The view takes my breath away,
It seems like I'm on top of the world,
I can see whatever I want.
I can see everything.

Amanda Gorecki
Age: 12

WHAT I LOVE ABOUT FOOTBALL

Football is what I love
The smell of grass and mud
The smell of sweat
The gear and the fear
Then the feeling before the game
The rush
The feeling of being the center of attention
The feeling of breaking tackles and tackling
The best feeling of all
Knows you are the undefeated champions

Brian DeLeonibus
Age: 12

ALWAYS WITH YOU

I want nothing more,
Than to be here with you,
I'll stay by your side,
And will always be true.
Whenever I'm sad,
With you
I'm now glad.
When I shed a tear,
You'll always come near.
I'll stay by your side,
'Til the day that you die.
Yes, this is all very true,
I'm so happy that I found you!

Chelsea Sebetich
Age: 12

MY DREAM

At night I stare at the sky,
The stars are bright,
The sky is clear,
Oh how dear,
The grass is green in my dream,
I dream and dream and dream,
To someday become a queen,
If only it could be more than a dream.

Crystal Lewis
Age: 12

THE UNCLE THAT I CHERISH

His time has come
The work has been done.
God's plan for him came,
Under the pouring rain.
Nighttime came and went
And so did he,
He was loved so much
I don't know how to explain it.
But when I gave him a hug,
I felt his touch.
He is with Jesus now,
As sad as it is,
He'd want us to be happy
Even though he is gone.
He is still in our hearts.
Day and night, night and day
Through the pouring rain.
Just remember when you see the sun,
Think of him looking down on us.
His time has come
The work has been done.

Hayley Canigiani
Age: 12

THE SKY

The sky is so beautiful,
It shines very bright.
When I look up,
At the clouds,
I see hundreds of pictures
Dancing through the sky,
Even when it's dark,
I look up at the stars,
Shining so very bright.

Ashley Carlson
Age: 13

THANKSGIVING

Thanksgiving is the time of year,
To be with the ones we hold so dear.
To share the day and have lots of fun,
To share a meal when the cooking is done,
Turkey with trimmings and pumpkin pie,
Are just a few reasons why,
We give thanks to God up above,
And thank Him for all His love.

Emily Krolik
Age: 12

THE HORSE

My horse is quite fast.
White and black spots cover him.
He likes to run free.

Naomi Bick
Age: 10

GONE

There's a girl who sighs
Looks to the skies
Blinks the tears from her eyes
Moves on
There's a girl who shouts
Lets the rage pour out
Is filled with doubt
Moves on
There's a girl who regrets
Refuses to accept
This she didn't expect
Moves on
There's a girl who sighs
Looks for you in the skies
Blinks the tears from her eyes
You're gone

Brandi Killian
Age: 14

FAMILY

F is for the fun we have together
A is for the awesome food we have on holidays
M is for the marvelous snowmen
  we build around Christmas
I is for the interesting stories my family tells
L is for all the love that is spread around
Y is for you'll love my family

No matter the family size, big or small,
a family is a family and you should love them all!!!

Alexa Rae Malesky
Age: 11

WINTER

Winter is such a beautiful time of the year,
Especially when the snow starts to fly.
You look out your window and all you see is white.
After the snow has fallen you can go sled riding,
If you have enough snow you can build a snowman.
When you're done playing in the snow and you are cold,
You can go inside to make some hot chocolate
to warm yourself up.
Winter is such a wonderful time of the year,
Christmas comes
and you get school days off from the snow!

April Mori
Age: 12

WINTER WOODLAND

In the glistening snow
We spotted a doe
We saw her graze
Behind a haze
A little over from the doe
In the snow we saw a rabbit
Get into a habit
Gnawing the glove
Beside the dove
As she flew I knew
I would never see her again

Haley Christine Yanko
Age: 10

I JUST REMEMBERED

I just remembered to get out of bed.
I just remembered to go out the bedroom door.
I just remembered to go down the stairs.
I just remembered to eat breakfast.
I just remembered to run out the door.
I just remembered to go to school!

Kieran Allen Loehr
Age: 6

A SUNNY DAY

'Twas the beginning of May
And I was sweeping the hay
That the horses had chewed.
As I swept I watched the flies they shoed.

Betsy, Shirley, Bob, Curly, and Pal
Are all the cows that we have now.
Betsy's calves Ben and Roo
Have no clue that they're cows of two.

Larry the rooster
Is quite the booster
Of all the hens that lay
'Cause we had breakfast with eggs today.

All the pigs are fat and lazy
But out of them all, my favorite is Mazy.
My second favorite pig is Belle
Her stomach is smooth and soft like gel.

Sheep are the quietest and softest of all
Also short, stubby, and not very tall.
Most of my clothes are made of wool
When sheep get shaved, they become very cool.

Smallest to tallest comes llamas
They are so cute I could put one in pajamas.
A llama can eat as much as a hog
But they also can be as fast as a dog.

Unlike the llama comes the goat
They're a lot smaller so they can swim and float.
When you get a goat glare
You need to be alert and to beware!

Turkeys are very strong and colorful
They're also chubby and blubberful.
All turkeys can be irritable
But they also can be fun.

Taller than llamas come ostriches
You might as well call them impostriches.
They will not do anything for me
They won't even eat a shrimpy flea.

After all the animals comes my whole family
And I love them on a sunny day.

Emma Morse
Age: 10

THE OCEAN

O ysters
C lown fish
E els
A ngelfish
N arrow-lined puffer fish

The ocean's where I like to be,
I have all the fishes swimming with me.

Marisa Kofmehl
Age: 10

WINTERTIME

In the winter, it's cold and white
It's fun to start a snowball fight
You can build a snowman or two
Put on the scarf and pull it tight
Add a carrot for the nose
And add some rocks for the toes
When the snow melts, the glee might be all over
But wait until next year comes and it will start all over!

Marissa Davis
Age: 12

CHRISTMAS

White all over on the ground
Snowflakes falling
The day is clear
People drinking hot cocoa
Kids making igloos
And having snowball battles
The trees are up
And ever so nice
Presents left by old Saint Nick
The previous night
For children of all ages
Excitement in the little faces
Reading Christmas stories
And spreading its cheer
Christmas is the best time of year

John Anderson
Age: 12

FALL

The frigid air gives me a chill,
While all the pumpkins are lined up still.
The blue sky is nice and clear,
That way I know fall is near.

All the leaves turn beautiful vibrant colors,
Come help rake them sisters and brothers.
Raking the leaves can also be fun,
Make a big pile and jump in everyone!

The scarecrow is up in the garden with care,
Hoping to give the big blackbirds a scare.
The garden is neatly planted line by line,
They will grow in time with water and shine.

Around the corner Thanksgiving will come,
You will need turkey so go get some.
Thanksgiving is about love and care,
Have a great fall everyone, everywhere!

Nicole Marie Miller
Age: 12

NATURE

As I look into the sky,
I see clouds rolling by,
Surrounded by a meadow of green,
Everything seems so serene.
The sounds of gentle animal chatter,
The soft fall of rain, pitter-patter.
The calm spray of the ocean breeze,
All of nature is at ease.

Marco Pugliese
Age: 11

BASEBALL

Baseball is my favorite sport.
I'd rather watch it,
Instead of basketball players
Running on a court.
Playing baseball
Is more important to me,
Than worrying about
Watching TV.
When I am playing baseball,
I don't worry
About having a great fall,
Or getting hit by a ball.
That is how I feel about baseball.

Thomas Seman
Age: 12

A TRIBUTE TO 9-11-2001

2001, on the eleventh of September,
a day that we all sadly remember.
On that day lots of courage was shown,
I'd like to honor some with a tribute of my own.

Here are some people who showed courage that day.
They helped to guide us in a very unique way.

The Firemen—
Fearlessly rushed into the Towers as brothers,
wanting to put out the fire, to save all the others.

The Police—
At the Towers and Pentagon working so hard,
bravely keeping all safe under their guard.

The Paramedics—
Working heroically all through the night,
digging through rubble—
Oh, what a fright!

The Workers—
Victims at all these targeted places,
with courage showing on their faces.

The American People—
Moving on day to day we did try,
but all along we asked, "Why?"

The Injured—
I acknowledge their long courageous fight,
to recover from injuries they got that night.

All Who Died—
In the Trade Center, Pentagon and Flight 93,
their courage burns bright in the land of the free!

Megan Gramm
Age: 12

SNOW

S o cold you can get frostbite
N ever-ending blanket
O n the ground
W hite and sparkling

Audrey Filey
Age: 8

DANCING

I am really happy when I am dancing.
Dancing is fun when you've got all the moves.
The music is playing and you get in the groove.
My feet start dancing; there's so much to prove.
All across the dance floor, I begin to cruise.
It doesn't matter the color of your skin,
With dancing everyone fits in.
I know you can do it, there's nothing to lose.
So don't just sit there, come on and dance.
It's really fun, just give it a chance.
Ballet, jazz, hip-hop or tap,
You can even choose to rap.
It's fun, it's cool.
You can even dance at school.
It's time to get up,
There's no time to sit,
Start dancing and moving
And get physically fit.

Jacquelyn Zumbo
Age: 11

Sunrise, sunset
Like a mural painted in the sky
A couple of minutes and the loveliness goes by
Sunrise, sunset
Marks the beginning
Marks the end
And everything is quiet
Sunrise, sunset
You see the colors
Through the trees
And now it seems
As if it's the only peaceful thing anyone sees
Sunrise, sunset
Like a mural painted in the sky
A couple minutes and the loveliness goes by
And time stops

Charlotte Harris
Age: 12

MY ARMY DAD

I love you a lot
And I know you do too
Which I already know
It's just me and you
It sometimes is hard
When you are away
But I want you to know
I think of you every day
I miss you a lot
I can’t wait 'til you're home
So we can play again
Instead of talking on the phone
Me and you
Playing together
You are my daddy
And will always be forever

Jackie Lin Asbury
Age: 11

MY TEACHER

Sometimes my teacher is like the weather,
I think she will be that way forever.
At times she can be a thunderstorm,
And she will yell, "It is not very warm!"

Sometimes she can be a rainy day,
And be droopy and sad all the way.
Sometimes she can be like the hail,
"Do your homework, or you will fail!"

Most of the time she can be sunny,
And be very bright and really funny.
So, if you're unsure as you go past,
Come into our room for the weather forecast.

Madison Moro
Age: 11

A FLYING AVALON

Up above the clouds so high,
Lies a city in the sky.
With sparkling lights,
It's full of delights.
To every eye, it'll let out a sigh . . .
Of sparkling dust,
And twittering wings,
Only to be found through fairy rings.
Of rubenesque gnomes,
And mushroom domes,
Of prancing ponies,
And dancing cronies,
Of singing sirens,
And rocks where merpeople are a-lying.
But come past the midnight hour,
This city will have lost its magical power.
Again, this joy will come,
But not until the next day is done.

Morganna Becker
Age: 13

THE OPEN HIGHWAY

I'm standin' alone.
It's a drowsy day.
I'm lookin' forward,
On the open highway.
It gives me hope,
But also fear.
My life begins with me standin' here.
I wanna think,
My life to be easy.
But, for some reason,
It's just so hard.
I look through the glass,
And I see it clearly.
My life's story has just begun.

Anna J. Sabo
Age: 12

SCHOOL

I love to come to school,
It's the best place to be.
It's a place,
Where you can get away from the parents.
It's a place you go,
To see people or friends.
Another thing you go to school for,
Education so you can get a good job.
You have a whole bunch of teachers,
They all teach a different subject.
School is sometimes fun,
But then sometimes not fun.
It depends on what you do that day.
School can be fun if you make it that way.

Kristen Lees
Age: 12

You see me in the hall,
and smile when you walk by.
You make me so confused,
why can't you be my guy?

You treat me like I'm special,
and make me feel anew.
But I just can't help and wonder,
do you like me as I like you?

You put your arm around me,
and get that twinkle in your eye.
I get a really special feeling,
but what does it signify?

I like you and I need to know
just what you feel for me.
I think we could have something more;
please just tell me you agree.

Sarah Karg
Age: 15

CHRISTMASTIME

Christmas is my favorite time of year.
  Everyone is full of cheer.
Friends and family gather from far and near,
  and when driving they watch for reindeer.
There might be some ice, so watch your step.
  The best is still yet to come.
When Christmas Eve rolls around,
  be careful not to make a sound.
If the reindeer hear a noise,
  you may not get all your toys.
When you wake up on Christmas Day,
  check to see if the reindeer ate their hay.
Opening presents is lots of fun,
  but I'm sad when it is done.

Stacey Bonasorte
Age: 12

NO REGRETS

It seemed the world was crashing down,
I couldn't smile I could only frown,
My days of fun done for a little while anyway,
Now I feel like I weigh a ton,
I did what I shouldn't have done
I did it but I won't say it wasn't fun.
I'll deal with the consequences,
But you'll see me next year throwing the eggs,
And jumping the fences
Some people call it destruction
I say it's just a kid's way to function
Many times my mom would say not to throw eggs
I wasn't listening now I'm here with two fractured legs
Once I tossed two eggs ran towards a fence
Jumped down and I felt very tense
Now I sit here telling myself no regrets

Justin Sellew
Age: 13

THE STORY OF A BUNNY

There once was a bunny, a silly "clown."
Who wore kiss-me T-shirts
and polka-dot boxers to town.
He needed money,
But he wasn't very funny,
So he stole the Queen of England's crown.

He sold the diamond crown on E-bay,
Then bought a house by the San Francisco Bay.
He bought it for a million,
But sold the crown for a zillion,
Because he needed that
to buy his vacation home in Pompeii.

The bunny got into trouble, this time it was bad.
The queen arrested him, which made him very sad.
He was put into jail,
With his little pet snail
And that act made his mother very, very mad.

The bunny was in jail for more than a year
'Til his mother bailed him out, and set his priorities clear.
He went to see the queen,
After the ten cups of caffeine
And made the queen so mad that she started to tear.

To this day no one has seen the bunny.
Some say she had him with milk and honey.
One thing is for sure,

She slammed the door,
And took all of the bunny's precious, little money.

The queen got her diamond crown back
After the many hours spent which tightened her back.
When the crown was delivered,
Everyone ran downriver,
Because she dropped it and made it crack.

Sydney Rusak
Age: 12

Very good jumpers
Cats are one of the best pets
Wonderful hunters

Jordan Kester
Age: 8

SUMMERTIME

On a summer day
We ride away.
In the car
It seems so far.
We got there
And breathed beach air.
Sea gulls in the sky.
They flew right by.
We ran to the sea
With happiness and glee.
I wanted to swim in the ocean.
Mom said I needed suntan lotion.
I ran up the beach
And ate a ripe peach.
I sat on the sand
And drew with my hand.
I looked at the sun.
Summer had just begun.

Gabrielle Kosobucki
Age: 8

A FALL DAY

It was a dark, cold morning.
The weather outside was storming.
The leaves were wet and cold.
You could see the red, orange, yellow and gold.
I looked out the window at the park.
The trees were very scary and dark.
The wind blew the leaves all around.
They were nearly ten feet off the ground.
It was not a good day to go outside.
So I stayed in my bed and decided to hide.

Kathryn Olon
Age: 8

THE EAGLE

The eagle flies so very high,
  Up into the big, blue sky.
His wings fly out so very far,
  They're almost as big as a car.
The eagle likes to hunt his prey,
  He does this almost every day.
The eagle is so very cool,
  Learn about him at your school.

Kayla Ventura
Age: 10

A WINTER DAY

I wake up in the morning and what do I see?
All the snowflakes falling like crazy.
The ground is frozen, white all around.
We build a snowman so smooth and round.
The air is cold, crisp and clear.
I walk quickly; my destination is near.
I skate and play hockey on the frozen lake.
My mom says, "Be careful the ice might break!"
I go out there with no worries at all.
I skate like I walk; I don't ever fall.
This is my favorite time of the year.
I am scoring goals, hockey is here.

Andrew Gaus
Age: 9

Puppies jumping over pans
Dumping cans
Having fun
Eating buns

Danielle Patterson
Age: 8

MY CHRISTMAS STORY

I went to bed on Christmas Eve,
So, Santa wouldn't have to leave,
I hoped for presents under the tree,
The things that I wanted them to be,
Like candy canes and turtlenecks,
And maybe a few card decks,
For Santa I've left some cookies and cheese,
Now bring me some presents, please, oh please,
My dreams are filled with candy canes,
And frosty-white windowpanes,
Please, bring me some treats,
Please make most of them sweets,
Our stockings are filled with presents galore,
Because of Santa who we adore,
This Christmas was filled with glory,
But, this is the real Christmas story,
In a manger he sleeps and lays,
Baby Jesus, born this day.

Rachel Lapp
Age: 10

LOVE

How do you know when you're in love?
Is it when your heart beats faster and faster
when you are with that person?
Or is it when you can't stop thinking
about that one special person
And you can't wait to talk to them
even if it's just for a simple hello?
Can you really even tell when you're in love?
Is it something you just realize
the first time you see that person?
Do you have to wait awhile to find out?
How do you know you'll even fall in love?
Or how do you know
there's even that one special person out there for you?
I guess you just have to live life and find out yourself.

Melinda Siber
Age: 13

IN THE FUTURE

In the future,
I'll be something special.
Something that makes a difference in the world.
Or, maybe someone.
I'll try to do good deeds.
I'll try to be someone that can help with anything.
Or maybe a special something,
Something that's not seen every day,
Something that's not there all of the time,
Something that is made from your heart,
Not your appearance.
I know I will be someone special.
I know I'll do something special.
But until then, I'll do what I can now.
By helping.
Just helping anyone.
I'll do what I can.

Brad Hammer
Age: 14

WATERFALLS

Roar, splash, pound
Just look at it flow,
Like a blanket over the ground,
Crashing water down below.

Ian Kelly
Age: 11

The yellow sun
I'm going out to play
Beating down as I run
What a wonderful day!

Lane C. Ward
Age: 8

HERO

You are
respectful,
kind, and caring.
You treat
everyone like
they are their
own individual.
You stand out
among the crowd.
You can conquer
anything you
dream.
You are everything
I want in a
friend.
You are my
hero.

Lauren Meuschke
Age: 13

America is the place where everyone's free
No matter what you look like
America is where you can practice
The religion of your choice
America is the most powerful nation on earth
And proud of it
America is where you can say anything you want
And not be punished
America is where the rules always stay the same
America is where we can feel safe in times of war
And in times of peace
America is the role model for the world
And will carry on that reputation into the future
America is where your potential is endless
Only if you try
America is where freedom rings

Ryan Alan
Age: 13

Student
attentive, ready
learning, exploring, experimenting
capable, talented--patient, intelligent
teaching, helping, guiding
helpful, kind
Teacher

Nicole Klacic
Age: 13

Trees
falling
lots of leaves
a lot of shade
Fall

Kayla Angeline
Age: 8

THE STORM

As I stand by the pond, I gaze,
gaze out upon the shimmering waters,
upon the trees, towering high above the surface.
Deer leap in the background.
Birds sing as they fly
high above my head.
All the beauty of the earth,
summoned to the spot on which I stand.

Suddenly, the sky darkens.
The birds and beasts scatter,
but the beauty never leaves.
A new beauty appears.
I see it in the swirling, gray clouds,
in the black, velvety waters churning,
as the trees dance around me.

I sit and watch
the storm.

Samantha Bergman
Age: 13

ESCAPING FROM REALITY

I wish I could just float away
and escape from everyday life.
I wish I could go to someplace special
where I could be alone.
I wish I knew of a place
where the sun shined every day.
I wish I knew of a place
where I could let my sorrows flee from my mind.
I wish I could let all my thoughts float away,
float away like leaves in the breeze.
I wish I could let the stress escape from my mind
while I lie back and count all the stars in the sky.
As I lay my head down,
and start to fall asleep,
I let my thoughts drift away,
as I dream of my ideal place.
I wish my special place were real.
I wish that I could escape to it,
but for now,
dreaming will have to do.

Alexis Green
Age: 13

SPORTS

I play sports all year long,
  On a field or a court is where I belong.
Soccer, baseball, and basketball are what I play,
  If we win I'll feel good at the end of the day.
In baseball I swing the big heavy bat,
  I love the dirt on my pants and the sweat in my hat.
Next comes basketball, it is another great sport,
  I feel the thrill when I'm dribbling down the court.
Finally, soccer, it's the greatest of all,
  I enjoy running, kicking, and fighting for the ball.
Did I make my point? Now can you see?
  That anything but sports is just not for me.

Bryan L. Demyan
Age: 13

Dogs so big
Running so fast for a test
Such dirt diggers
Simply the best

Casum Matlick
Age: 9

THE ESSENCE OF FLY-FISHING

Rivers, streams, waters all,
Through winter, spring, summer, and fall.
Many anglers had their try,
But few have done it with a fly.

A small lure, gently tied,
And many kinds are often tried.
But the fly itself does not come last,
What comes next is the cast.

One jerk forward is all it takes,
To send the fly over the ponds and lakes.
Landing gently on the surface,
Seemingly without a purpose.

All is quiet for the moment,
But now the rod shows some movement.
This is what fly-fishing is all about,
Using tiny flies to catch huge trout.

David William Hazen
Age: 14

THE WOODS

I live in the woods
and I like it that way.
You never know what animals
you'll see in a day.
Some days you see turkeys,
some days you see deer.
That's what makes it so great
to live here.
I can ride my quad,
I can go for a hike,
I can do just about
anything that I like.
We have a lot of acres,
fifty-three you see.
That really lets
me be free.
So if you ever
want to run, jump and fall,
just give me a call,
we can do it all.

Johnnie Noftz

THE LONG AND WINDY ROAD

Paul McCartney, John Lennon, George Harrison,
and Ringo Starr,
Oh did they come far.
Originally from Liverpool, England,
They would soon become famous in all states
especially New England.
They wrote "Hey Jude,"
It would instantly change the mood.
One of their songs "Sgt. Pepper's Lonely Heart Band,"
Was listened to all across the land.
At times it was sad,
but their music remained rad.
They wrote "Come Together,"
But deaths made them say fare weather.

Samuel Miclot
Age: 12

ICE CREAM

Ice cream is sweet,
Ice cream is yummy,
Ice cream is good in your tummy.
Vanilla, chocolate, strawberry. Wow!
Any more? You like it how.
Oh moose tracks, cookie dough, sherbet too,
As long as you get it it doesn't matter to you!
Save some for me for I like it too!

Courtney Kovick
Age: 10

I DIDN'T DO MY HOMEWORK

"I didn't do my homework for today,"
Said little Lizzy Izzylay.
"Because my sister caught her hair on fire
And my dog got caught in barbed wire.
I was playing outside,
and my soccer ball rolled down the street
Faster than I could run with my feet."
"Well, why were you outside when you should have
been doing homework, your first task?"
Mrs. Jones, our teacher, asked.
"Let me finish my sympathetic tale!"
Lizzy said with a wail.
"We got in the car,
but we got stuck in wet tar.
Curious, I stepped out,
Only to hear a shout.
'Get off there you fool!
The road is not yet cool!'
I jumped back in surprise,
And quickly said my good-byes.
On the way back,
Our car must have run over a very large tack.
For the car was leaning to the right,
But my mom just said, 'It's all right.
Let's just get out to see what's wrong.'
Mom hesitated then said,
'It looks like we won't be zooming right along.'
Then there, right in front of me, was a flat tire!
Now we were dire.
Home is so far away I thought,
To get home we will have to walk A LOT!

Finally once we were back at our house,
My little brother said, 'I found a mouse,
His name is Brett.
Can I please keep him as a pet?'
Mom and I looked at each other,
And thought oh brother.
She yelled, 'NO!'
He just walked out of the room sad and slow.
Then I was about to do my homework for you,
I heard my dad yell in pain, 'SUE!'
My mom ran to find him.
He was holding his limb.
His hammer was sprawled out on the floor,
And his finger looked sore.
Dad stammered,
'I nailed myself with the hammer.'
While Dad went to the emergency room,
I thought better do my homework I assume.
But then it started to thunderstorm really bad.
Since it was dark--I couldn't find my writing pad.
Oh! I forgot to say,
The power went off--to my dismay.
So as you can see,
My day was filled with no glee.
There was no time for school stuff,
And believe me this is no bluff!"
"Lizzy, the homework was not due today,"
Mrs. Jones said.
"Just remember, tonight, write an essay."
Lizzy said happily, "Oh, it's not?
Cool, then I just forgot."

Katie Stack

THE DAY BEFORE VACATION

The day before vacation,
I cannot fall asleep,
There was a great threat to our nation,
For many people weep.

Our hearts are filled with sadness,
Watching brothers and sisters in pain,
We pray to God to stop this madness,
And heal us with a peaceful rain.

It's time for us to come together,
As we all sing out loud,
Let it be known for now and forever,
For we are the U.S.A. and we are proud.

Zack Evans
Age: 12

NEVER GIVING UP

Every time you feel
Like giving up
You feel like throwing in the towel
From all this buildup

You don't know what to do
Because you aren't sure
But, you can't give up
You must endure

You shouldn't have to worry
And you shouldn't have to cry
You've got to spread your wings
You've got to dare to fly

Rachel Kost
Age: 12

ONLY SEVEN

I wish
That life would last forever.
But,
By doing so I would never grow
To understand
Why you couldn't stay to hold my hand.

You were sick,
And that was fine.
You would always be there.
And you would make me smile
Every time.

Then you left,
You had to go,
It was Saturday morn,
When you left me alone.

You moved to Georgia,
Sad, but true
I was nothing without you.

You got sicker,
I didn't know.
Then that one sad day came . . .

I heard the news,
You died,
Just that night.

A little girl,
Only seven.
Lost her life,
And went to
Heaven.

Carly Krystyniak
Age: 13

FALL

I was walking near the trees
When I felt a cool breeze.
The leaves were crunching
When I heard someone munching.
It was a squirrel up in a tree.
It was eating and staring at me.
I was off to the store
To get pumpkins galore.
I gave them all faces
And put them in different places.
Then I lay down my head
At last I went to bed.

Samantha Mack
Age: 8

TEACHERS

Guess who teaches? Guess who teaches?
Ms. Paula Pellafone teaches!
Ms. Paula Pellafone teaches poems!
She teaches fifth graders.
She is a really nice teacher in fifth grade!

Guess who teaches? Guess who teaches?
Mrs. Mary Atta Filotei teaches!
Mrs. Mary Atta Filotei teaches math!
She teaches fifth graders.
She is a really nice teacher in fifth grade!

Guess who teaches? Guess who teaches?
Mrs. Linell Cagno teaches reading!
She teaches education to kids.
She is a really nice teacher!

Guess who teaches? Guess who teaches?
Mrs. Matey teaches!
Mrs. Matey teaches art!
She is a really nice teacher!

Guess who teaches? Guess who teaches?
Ms. Bock teaches!
Ms. Bock is a librarian!
She is a really nice teacher!

Guess who teaches? Guess who teaches?
Mr. Fedigin teaches!
Mr. Fedigin teaches physical education!
He is a really nice teacher!

Guess who teaches? Guess who teaches?
Mrs. Olsen teaches.
Mrs. Olsen teaches music
She is a really nice teacher!

Guess who teaches? Guess who teaches?
Mr. Gittens teaches!
Mr. Gittens teaches us about computers!
He is a really nice teacher!

Brooke Zivkovich
Age: 10

LITTLE BROWN LEAF

The tree is so green
But has one little brown leaf
It ruins it all

Adam Benson
Age: 13

A DAY OF MISERY

It was such a bad day,
And it stayed that way.
When my teacher had told me what happened,
I was confused but frightened.
I wondered how that could be.
She told me that the World Trade Center
had been knocked down,
I just stood there and made no sound.
I thought of all the people that died,
And their families didn't have a chance to say good-bye.
As I stood there,
I began to cry,
And the sad thing was, it wasn't a lie.

Regina Marie Aluise
Age: 12